W9-BNN-500

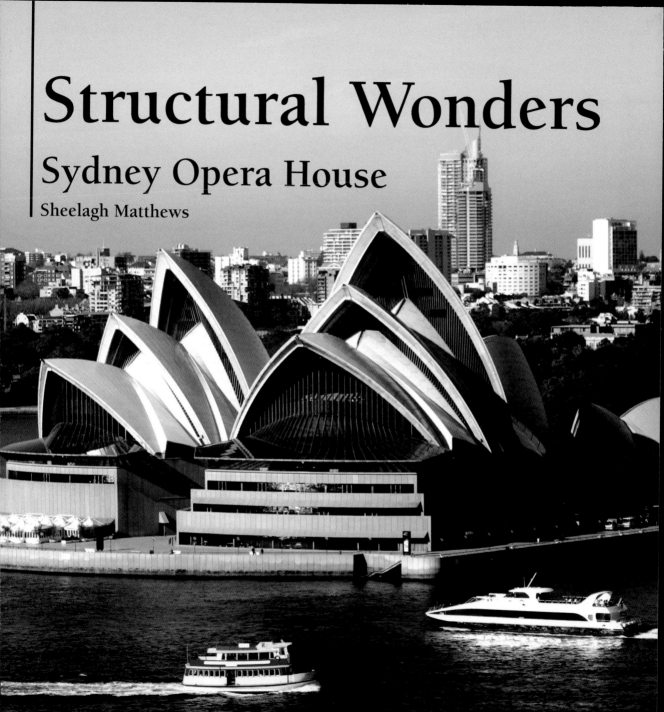

Structural Wonders

Sydney Opera House

Sheelagh Matthews

Published by Weigl Publishers Inc.
350 5th Avenue, Suite 3304, PMB 6G
New York, NY 10118-0069

Website: www.weigl.com

Library of Congress Cataloging-in-Publication Data

Matthews, Sheelagh.
 The Sydney Opera House / Sheelagh Matthews.
    p. cm. – (Structural Wonders)
 Includes index.
 ISBN 978-1-59036-936-4 (hard cover: alk. Paper) –
 ISBN 978-1-59036-937-1 (soft cover: alk. Paper) (N.S.W.) –
 Buildings, structures, etc. – Juvenile literature. I. Title.
 NA6840.A79S95 2009
 725'.822099441—dc22

2008015667

Printed in the United States of America
1 2 3 4 5 6 7 8 9 0 12 11 10 09 08

Photograph Credits

Weigl acknowledges Getty Images as its primary image supplier.

Peter Guthrie: page 11 bottom

Every reasonable effort has been made to trace ownership and to obtain
permission to reprint copyright material. The publishers would be pleased
to have any errors or omissions brought to their attention so that they may
be corrected in subsequent printings.

All of the internet URLs given in the book were valid at the time of publication.
However, due to the dynamic nature of the Internet, some addresses may have
changed, or sites may have ceased to exist since publication. While the author
and publisher regret any inconvenience this may cause readers, no responsibility
for any such changes can be accepted by either the author or the publisher.

Project Coordinators: Heather C. Hudak, Heather Kissock
Design: Terry Paulhus

Contents

What is the Sydney Opera House?

With its gigantic white sails and its picturesque setting, the Sydney Opera House has captured the imagination of the world. Considered an architectural wonder, this structure is a reminder of Australia's coming of age. It was built ahead of its time in terms of style and available technology.

Poised on the tip of Bennelong Point in Sydney Harbour, the Sydney Opera House looks like a great ship that is about to set sail. This monumental structure is a feat of innovation and teamwork in engineering, design, and construction.

The Sydney Opera House is a world-class performing arts centre, a tourist attraction, and a place to hold community events. Its design includes three structures of interlocking, **vaulted** shells. The shells house the two main performance venues, a 1,507-seat Opera Theatre and 2,679-seat Concert Hall. The forecourt holds up to 6,000 people for special outdoor concerts and festivals. A restaurant for fine dining, many smaller performance venues, and meeting rooms add to the vibrancy of the complex.

Jutting out into one of the most beautiful natural harbors in the world, the Sydney Opera House greets people from the land, sea, and air. The brilliant-white roof shells of the Sydney Opera House have become an **icon** and a national symbol of Australia.

Quick Bites
- The Sydney Opera House hosts almost 3,000 events each year. About two million people attend these shows. Another 200,000 visitors take guided tours each year.
- It takes about 650 staff to operate the Sydney Opera House.

Building History

The idea for the Sydney Opera House came shortly after World War II. At this time, Australia wanted to become well known around the world for its cultural offerings. In 1956, a design competition to build an opera house in Sydney, a major Australian city, was announced.

Architects around the world submitted more than 200 design proposals to compete in this important project. It was a fresh, **innovative** design by Jørn Utzon of Denmark that won the hearts of the judges and the public.

Jørn left the project before it was complete, and he has never returned to Australia.

Construction on Utzon's **tiered**-roof design began in 1959. His concept challenged traditional views of construction. It required the use of new technologies and materials. Helping to develop the construction strategy was Ove Arup & Partners, a **structural engineering** firm. With so many challenges to overcome, construction took much longer and cost more than planned. Project delays and increased costs caused many people to become upset with Utzon. To save costs and time, many of Utzon's original plans for the structure's interiors were left out of the structure.

Construction on the Sydney Opera House cost about 10 times more than had been budgeted for the project.

TIMELINE OF CONSTRUCTION

1952: The government of New South Wales, a state of Australia, decides to build an opera house.

1954: The Opera House Committee is formed. Bennelong Point in Sydney Harbour is chosen as the site.

1956: An international design competition is announced.

1957: Danish-born architect, Jørn Utzon, is declared the winner of the opera house design competition.

1959–1973: Construction of the opera house complex takes place.

October 20, 1973: Queen Elizabeth II declares the Sydney Opera House open.

Utzon's son, Jan Utzon, also worked on the Sydney Opera House 25th anniversary plans.

Others stepped into complete the building. On October 20, 1973, a celebration was held, and Queen Elizabeth II declared the Sydney Opera House open. It took 14 years and $102 million Australian dollars to build the modern-looking monument.

Many changes have been made to the Sydney Opera House over the years. In 1979, the largest mechanical pipe organ in the world was installed in the Concert Hall. In 1993, an underground parking lot was added. For its 25th anniversary in 1998, Australian architect Richard Johnson was asked to work on designs for future work on the opera house.

Johnson suggested that the original architect, Jørn Utzon, be hired to work on the project as well. After long talks, Utzon agreed to once again work on his best-known design. He described the original concept for the structure and the site. Some of his designs were added to the building. In 2004, the Reception Hall was renovated to meet Utzon's original design. It was renamed the Utzon Room in his honor.

The Sydney Opera House is one of the busiest performing arts centers in the world.

Structural Wonders

The Sydney Opera House often is called the eighth wonder of the world.

Big Ideas

With its billowing, concrete sails, the Sydney Opera House is an expression of artistic vision. It took engineering genius and many years of effort and hard work. Jørn Utzon's design concept for the Sydney Opera House was unlike anything that had ever been built before. Architecture, engineering, sculpture, landscape design, and urban design were all major elements in the structure's success.

When drawing up his plans, Utzon wanted to take advantage of the site's beautiful natural setting on the water and its backdrop of urban skyscrapers. To do this, he used natural, organic forms to create the reflective vaulted roof shells. The roof shells look like the wedges of an orange and the scales of a fish. Utzon contrasted these organic structures by placing them on top of a vast, stepped platform. The platform, called the "podium," was inspired by ancient Mayan temples in Mexico.

Utzon's design included a new approach to theater design. He wanted to separate the performing arts centers from the behind-the-scenes needs. To do this, the two main performing arts centers, the Concert Hall and the Opera Theatre, were placed on top of the massive podium. All of the backstage and technical equipment were hidden within the podium. In total, the complex has more than 1,000 rooms. Most of these rooms are inside the podium.

Web Link:
To find out more about the beautiful natural harbor where the Sydney Opera house sits, visit www.livingharbour. net/index.cfm.

1) The Sydney Opera House is considered to be an "urban sculpture." 2) Jørn Utzon wanted the roof of the Sydney Opera House to look like the sails of a ship. 3) The tallest group of shells houses the Concert Hall and rises about 20 stories high above the water. The center shells house the Opera Theatre. The smallest shells contain a restaurant for fine dining.

Profile:
Jørn Utzon

The architect who designed the Sydney Opera House was a young man hailing from halfway around the world. Born in Copenhagen, Denmark, Jørn Utzon was only 38 years old when his design concept won the a competition for an opera house in Sydney, Australia. In 1957, Utzon's design of vaulted roof shells was selected out of 233 entries. He was not expected to win the contest, as his entry was not complete. He submitted rough drawings for review, and he changed this concept many times as the structure was being built.

Jørn Utzon was born into a family of sailors. His father was an esteemed ship builder who taught his son how to design ideas, draw plans, and make models. In high school, Utzon learned how to sculpt, and he decided to become an artist. He began studying at Copenhagen's Royal Academy of Arts in 1937. Soon, he discovered he had a talent for designing structures. In 1942, he graduated with a gold medal for architecture. This was the first of many awards he received for his work. Following his studies, Utzon spent the next 10 years traveling and working in many parts of the world, including Europe, Australia, Japan, India, Mexico, and the United States.

OTHER ARCHITECTURE BY UTZON

Kingo Housing Project
Utzon won the Ecksenberg Medal for Architecture in 1957 for this courtyard-style housing project. All of the 63 houses are L-shaped, follow the shape of the land, and are placed in the best possible positions for views, sunlight, and shelter from the wind.

Kuwait National Assembly Complex
Built out of concrete, Kuwait's legislature is a striking building of hanging fabric-like curves. The structure includes a parliamentary chamber, a covered square, a conference hall, and a mosque.

Utzon has never seen the Sydney Opera House in person.

In 1937, Utzon married Lis Fenger, a Danish commercial artist. Together, they had two sons, Jan and Kim, and one daughter, Lin. Jan and Kim followed their father's footsteps and became architects. Lin, an artist, is known for her work in designing porcelain murals, vases, and other art pieces.

In 1956, Utzon began working on his entry for the Sydney Opera House design competition. After being announced the winner, he worked on the project in Denmark until 1963, making visits each year to Sydney. In early 1963, Utzon moved his family to Sydney to continue his work on the project. However, due to problems with construction delays and cost overruns, Utzon left the project in 1966.

Still, Utzon's career as an architect continued to blossom. He was hired to design more buildings, including the Kuwait National Assembly Complex and the Bagsvaerd Church. In 2003, Jørn Utzon won the Pritzker Architecture Prize. Winning this award is the one of the highest honors an architect can receive.

Bagsvaerd Church

Utzon was hired to design a new church for Bagsvaerd, a town located north of Copenhagen in Denmark. From the outside, the church looks somewhat uninteresting. Its interior, however, is stunning. It features vaulted, curved ceilings that were inspired by clouds.

Can Feliz (Utzon home)

Can Feliz is a vacation home that Utzon built on the island of Majorca. Nestled on the side of a mountain, it has been described as a miniature **acropolis**. Can Feliz uses one of Utzon's favorite architectural concepts—the platform.

The Science Behind the Building

The construction of the Sydney Opera House was a rare and outstanding architectural achievement. Building it required special construction methods and materials. Many engineers, building contractors, architects, and manufacturers had to work together.

Spherical Geometry

The most challenging part of building the Sydney Opera House was the construction of the unique vaulted roof shells. It took four years to come up with a plan for building them. Utzon's inspiration was an orange that had been cut up into pieces. He used the pieces to see how the roof shells should be put together.

Utzon used a sphere as a model for the roof shells. He gave each shell the same amount of **curvature**. This meant all of the shell exteriors would have a clearly defined **geometry** in common. In fact, if all of the pieces of the roof of the Sydney Opera House were put together, they would form a sphere. This use of spherical geometry made it possible for the shell components to be **prefabricated** and mass produced.

In all, 2,194 precast concrete roof sections were used on the Sydney Opera House. They were installed, like building blocks, with the use of cranes. As well, 1,056,000 ceramic roof tiles were mass produced.

Visual Effects

The glossy white roof tiles of the Sydney Opera House reflect the sky. They take on many looks between sunrise and sunset every day. To create this effect, two types of tile finishes were used, one glossy and one **matte**.

The tiles were placed on the body of the shells in a geometrical pattern, giving them a fishbone look. To contrast the large, glossy roof areas, matte tiles were placed along the shell edges. This made the building look as though it had ribs. Without this contrast between glossy and matte tiles, the roof shells would have looked like huge, flat surfaces. When light hits the tiles, this contrast gives the building definition, depth, and reflection.

The Properties of Glass

With 67,005 square feet (6,225 meters) of glass in the structure, the **properties** of glass had to be accounted for when the Sydney Opera House was designed. Solar energy can readily pass through glass, raising the temperature inside the enclosure. This is known as the greenhouse effect. Glass also conducts sound, which can be a problem in a noisy harbor.

Web Link:
To view floor plans and photos of the Sydney Opera House under construction, visit www.gids.nl/sydney/opera.html

To deal with potential heat and sound transfer problems, a special type of glass was made. Two layers of this glass stop the sound of ships from affecting performances in the halls. These layers also help **insulate** the structure from the heat of the Sun's rays.

Science and Technology

Heavy lifting is a large part of building construction. Sydney Opera House workers relied on cranes to raise and install heavy concrete roof sections. To prepare the site for construction, more than 39,238 cubic yards (30,000 cubic m) of rock and rubble had to be removed from Bennelong Point in Sydney Harbour. This feat was done using mechanical shovels.

Hydraulics

A hydraulic system has two pistons in cylinders filled with an incompressible liquid, often oil. The oil is pumped to the cylinders and pistons through valves. The pistons are connected by a pipe. When pressure is applied to one piston, the force is transferred to the second piston through the oil. As one piston is pushed down, the other is lifted by the oil. This back-and-forth movement powers the machine. Hydraulics systems are highly flexible because the pipe connecting the pistons can be of any length. It can even be bent to fit around corners. The incompressible oil will still move the pistons. Changing the size of one piston and cylinder creates even more force and power.

Hydraulic shovels use two pistons—one at the elbow of the shovel's arm and another to turn the bucket. These pistons work with motors to operate the digging and rotating motion of the shovel.

Hydraulic shovels can weigh nearly 30 tons (27 tonnes) and can remove more than 35 cubic feet (1 cubic m) of dirt at a time.

Pulleys

A pulley is a freely turning wheel with a grooved rim over which a belt or chain is guided. Pulleys help raise and lower heavy loads by changing the direction of a pulling force. Mechanical shovels use pulleys to do their job. In this case, a vehicle with a large bucket on a mechanical arm has a series of power-driven steel cables that run through pulleys to raise and lower the bucket. Cranes, machines that lift and move heavy construction materials and equipment into place, use pulleys to operate. Both pieces of machinery played large roles in building the Sydney Opera House.

Portland Cement and Reinforced Concrete

Portland cement works like a glue to hold the concrete together. It is the key ingredient used in most types of concrete. Concrete made from Portland cement is used to make dams, bridges, buildings, and pavement.

To make Portland cement, materials such as clay, limestone, and sand are crushed together and poured into a large oven called a kiln. The heat inside the kiln breaks down the materials, and they form new substances.

After it is removed from the kiln, the cement is mixed with water to produce concrete. Then, it is brought to the construction site in a special truck that has a rotating barrel. The barrel moves constantly to keep the concrete from hardening. Once poured, the surface of the concrete is kept damp so that it can **cure**, or harden. The longer the concrete is allowed to cure, the stronger it will be.

Reinforced bars, or rebar, are used to give concrete extra strength.

Concrete often needs help to stand up to strong forces. Reinforced concrete uses hidden metal bars to help it withstand the forces of compression, or squeezing, and tension, or pulling. The bars are placed inside the concrete mold. As the concrete cures, or dries, the bars bond to it.

Quick Bites

- When making Portland cement, the materials inside the kiln reach temperatures between 2,700° and 3,000° Fahrenheit (1,480° and 1,650° Celsius).
- Most modern structures are built using reinforced concrete. These structures can support 300 to 500 times their weight.

Computer-Aided Design

Architects are trained professionals who work with clients to design structures. Before anything is built, they make detailed drawings or models. These plans are important tools that help people visualize what the structure will look like. A blueprint is a detailed diagram that shows where all the parts of the structure will be placed. Walls, doors, windows, plumbing, electrical wiring, and other details are mapped out on the blueprint. Blueprints act as a guide for engineers and builders during construction.

For centuries, architects and builders worked without the aid of computers. Sketches and blueprints were drawn by hand. Highly skilled drafters would draw very technical designs. Today, this process is done using computers and sophisticated software programs. Architects use CAD, or computer-aided design, throughout the design process. Early CAD systems used computers to draft building plans. Today's computer programs can do much more. They can build three-dimensional models and computer simulations of how a building will look. They can also calculate the effects of different physical forces on the structure. Using CAD, today's architects can build more complex structures at lower cost and in less time.

Computer-aided design programs have been used since the 1960s.

The roof of the Sydney Opera House is its most notable feature.

Eye on Design

Building an Icon

Building an iconic structure is not an easy thing to do. Many of the design features included in the Sydney Opera House had never before been attempted in the construction industry. Often, one solution was dependent on the other.

One of the major challenges presented by the Sydney Opera House was the construction of the roof shells. With its unique harbor-side setting, Jørn Utzon wanted the roof of the Sydney Opera House to look like the sails of a ship. However, structures that looked like sails would also act like sails.

This meant the rigid roof shells might bend and break, or be pushed over, in strong winds. Utzon's challenge was to find a way to build concrete roof shells that could withstand the high winds of the sea. Teamwork and collaboration between the architect and the structural engineer resulted in a unique solution—an iconic structure with an unusually shaped precast concrete roof weighing 158,000 tons.

MEASURING THE OPERA HOUSE

Location

The Sydney Opera House is located on a peninsula, called Bennelong Point, in Sydney, Australia. Found in the scenic Sydney Harbour, the site is flanked by towering office buildings. It is also near the world's largest steel arch bridge, the Sydney Harbour Bridge. This bridge is known as Sydney's gateway to the Pacific Ocean.

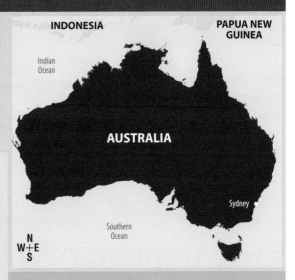

Height

The top peak of the Sydney Opera House is 220 feet (67 m) high.

Area

The buildings of the Sydney Opera House take up almost 5 acres (2 hectares) of land. The complex sits on a massive podium that is about 15 acres (6 hectares) in size. The structure is 607 feet (185 m) long and 394 feet (120 m) wide.

Weight

The Sydney Opera House weighs about 176,320 tons (160,000 tonnes). It sits on 580 concrete piers that extend underground to a depth of 82 feet (25 m).

Other Interesting Facts

- The mechanical pipe organ in the Concert Hall has 10,154 pipes.
- A lottery was held to help finance the Sydney Opera House. In November, 1957, tickets went on sale for about $10 Australian dollars (AU) each. First prize was about $200,000 (AU).

Environmental Viewpoint

The Sydney Opera House is surrounded by water on three sides. Directly behind the structure are the Royal Botanic Gardens, the city's "green lung." These natural elements provide some safety from growing urban development near the Sydney Opera House. However, the threat of development remains. In 2005, the Sydney Opera House was named a national landmark. It was given protected status when it was added to Australia's National Heritage List. A few years later, in 2007, it became a **UNESCO World Heritage Site**. Laws were put in place to ensure the Sydney Opera House would not be harmed by future development.

The building still faces other challenges. The side of the structure that faces the harbor is at risk of damage from environmental pressures. **Weathering** and pollution can be a problem for the structure. Winds can damage and remove tiles. Over time, this will degrade the frame of the building. The ebb and flow movement of the ocean puts pressure on the building's foundation. This causes cracks and chips that can become dangerous to the stability of the structure. Salty sea spray and runoff from **acid rain** can **erode** tiles and unprotected cement. Pollution, in the form of airborne chemicals, can erode unpainted concrete surfaces on the outside of the Sydney Opera House.

Thousands of people visit the Sydney Opera House each year.

The Australian government has been aware of these potential problems for many years. This led them to begin developing a conservation plan in 1993. With the help of Jørn Utzon and other advisors, the government believes it has a solid plan of action to keep the Sydney Opera House in excellent condition for years to come.

THE CONSERVATION PLAN

Over time, the Sydney Opera House has started to show signs of age and wear. It is important to ensure that is preserved for the future. In 2002, the government set aside more than 69 million Australian dollars for long-term care of the structure. As part of this funding, the former conservation plan was updated. The plan accounts for maintaining every part of the structure in a way that preserves Jørn Utzon's original design. Following the conservation plan helps make sure the site and structure are maintained to exceptional standards. The Conservation Plan also takes into consideration possible risks to the structure, such as pollution, overcrowding by people, and the sea's effect on the structure's base.

Construction Careers

Architects, engineers, carpenters, concrete workers, plumbers, electricians, stonemasons, crane operators, general laborers, and many others played an important role in the construction of the Sydney Opera House. Many of the design elements in this structure had never been attempted before. Those involved in building the Sydney Opera House used their knowledge, skills, and experience to find innovative solutions to construction challenges.

Structural Engineers

Structural engineers often work with architects, other engineers, and construction contractors. They help design load-bearing structures, such as roofs, bridges, towers, and buildings. They carry out inspections at different stages of the building process to make sure the structure can withstand different forces, such as wind, rain, and vibration. Structural engineers make sure structures are built safe, strong, and stable.

Concrete Finishers

Construction workers that specialize in concrete are called concrete finishers. They work both indoors and out, depending on the task. Concrete finishers pour wet concrete into casts, or molds, and spread it to a desired thickness. They level and smooth the surface and edges of the concrete. To give the concrete different effects, they apply various finishes to the surface. Using these finishes, they can give the concrete a smooth or patterned appearance. Concrete finishers also repair, waterproof, and restore concrete surfaces. This physical work involves lifting heavy bags of cement, bending, and kneeling. Concrete finishers must know how to age concrete perfectly in order for it to have maximum strength.

Landscape Architects

Landscape architects have both artistic and engineering talents, skills, and knowledge. The goal of a landscape architect is to create harmony between architectural structures and the site on which they are located. Landscape architects create, manage, and preserve environments so that they are both useful and look nice. They often work in a team environment, dealing with architects, urban planners, construction contractors, engineers, and, sometimes, environmental scientists. Landscape architects plan parks and help design green spaces to fit a building's design and use. They study the landscape of sites, including slope, plants, soil, and how water drains. Their landscape designs take into account social, economic, environmental, and artistic factors.

Web Link:
To find out more about concrete finishers, visit www.bls.gov/oco/ocos204.htm.

Notable Structures

Many different buildings have captured the attention of the world. Part of their appeal is the amount of effort and time involved in their construction. Mainly, however, it is the buildings appearance that draws people to it.

Parthenon

Built: 443 BC

Location: Athens, Greece

Design: Ictinus and Kallicrates

Description: The Parthenon is one of the best-known buildings on the Acropolis in Athens. With its mighty columns, the Parthenon is referred to as "the most perfect structure of **antiquity**." In ancient times, the Parthenon's purpose was to house the treasury of Athens, similar to modern-day banks.

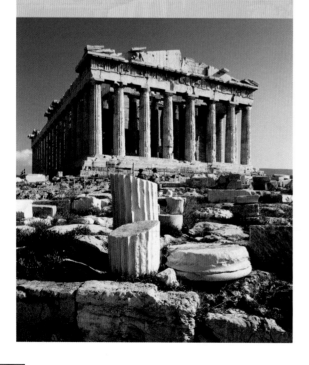

Taj Mahal

Built: 1653 AD

Location: Agra, India

Design: Mohammed Isa Afandi, Ustad Ahmed Lahori

Description: It took 20,000 laborers and the skill of many artists to build the Taj Mahal. This jewel-embedded **mausoleum** is known as a monument to eternal love. Shah Jahan built the Taj Mahal to contain the remains of his wife, Mumtaz Mahal.

Innovation in design and the effective use of materials have made certain buildings stand out throughout time in all parts of the world.

Solomon R. Guggenheim Museum

Built: 1959

Location: New York City, United States

Design: Frank Lloyd Wright

Description: This round-shaped building takes on a circle shape inside as well. It features oval-shaped columns and a huge concrete spiral walkway. To view the modern art inside, visitors start at the top of the walkway and work their way down.

Neuschwanstein Castle

Built: 1892

Location: Bavaria, Germany

Design: Christian Yank, Eduard von Riedel, Georg Dollman, Julius Hofmann

Description: This castle was built by Bavaria's King Ludwig II. It was modern for the time, as it included a central heating system and hot and cold running water. Walt Disney used this structure as the model for the castles in his theme parks.

Structural Icons Around the World

Structures that inspire the human imagination have been built all around the world. Some were built by ancient civilizations. Others were built in modern times.

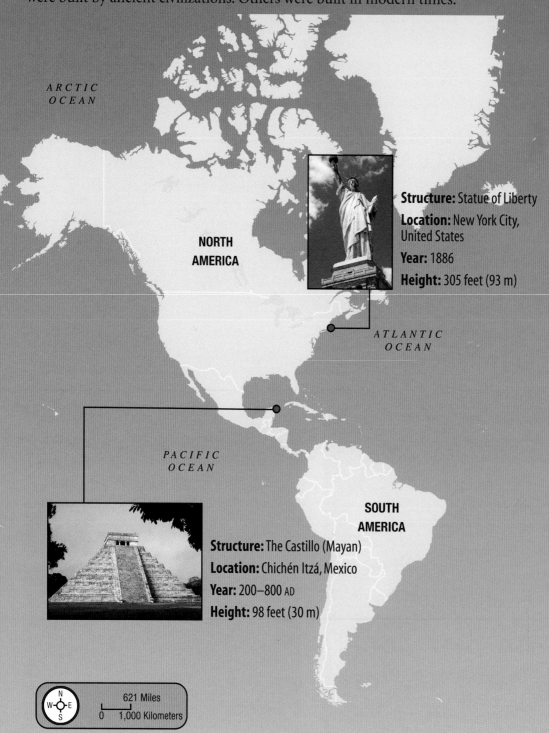

ARCTIC
OCEAN

**NORTH
AMERICA**

Structure: Statue of Liberty

Location: New York City,
United States

Year: 1886

Height: 305 feet (93 m)

ATLANTIC
OCEAN

PACIFIC
OCEAN

**SOUTH
AMERICA**

Structure: The Castillo (Mayan)

Location: Chichén Itzá, Mexico

Year: 200–800 AD

Height: 98 feet (30 m)

N
W–E
S

621 Miles

0   1,000 Kilometers

Many of these magnificent structures have become symbols or icons of nations.

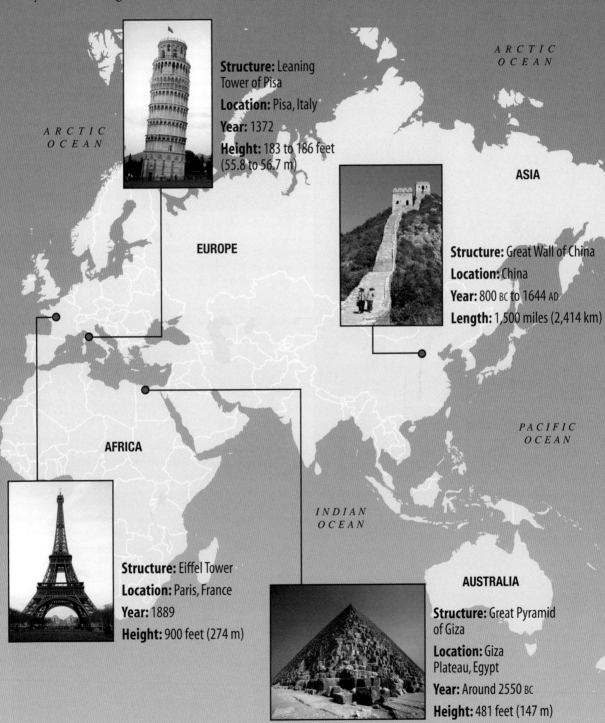

Structure: Leaning Tower of Pisa
Location: Pisa, Italy
Year: 1372
Height: 183 to 186 feet (55.8 to 56.7 m)

ARCTIC OCEAN

ARCTIC OCEAN

ASIA

EUROPE

Structure: Great Wall of China
Location: China
Year: 800 BC to 1644 AD
Length: 1,500 miles (2,414 km)

AFRICA

PACIFIC OCEAN

INDIAN OCEAN

Structure: Eiffel Tower
Location: Paris, France
Year: 1889
Height: 900 feet (274 m)

AUSTRALIA

Structure: Great Pyramid of Giza
Location: Giza Plateau, Egypt
Year: Around 2550 BC
Height: 481 feet (147 m)

Quiz

Q Where is the Sydney Opera House located?

A The Sydney Opera House is located in Bennelong Point, Sydney Harbour, Sydney, Australia.

Q Who designed the Sydney Opera House?

A Jørn Utzon designed the Sydney Opera House.

Q How many years did it take to build the Sydney Opera House?

A It took 14 years to build the Sydney Opera House.

Q What type of base is used for the Sydney Opera House?

A The Sydney Opera House was built on a platform, or "podium," an architectural concept used in the construction of Mayan pyramid temples.

Explore Spherical Geometry

Flat, or plane, geometry is the most common type of geometry. It deals with lines and triangles on flat surfaces. However, many types of surfaces are not flat. Some surfaces are curved like spheres. To measure a sphere, mapmakers, architects, and engineers use a type of geometry called spherical geometry.

Spherical geometry has some interesting differences from plane geometry. For example, in plane geometry, the angles within a triangle always add up to 180 degrees. In contrast, triangles on a curved or spherical surface can be greater than 180 degrees. Try this activity to see how different it can be to work in a spherical environment.

Instructions

1. Stand up. Let your arms hang down loosely beside your body.

2. Make a fist with your right hand. Leave your thumb sticking straight out. Your thumb should be pointing forward.

3. Keep your right arm straight, and do not twist your right wrist for the rest of the exercise.

4. Swing your right arm up and out to the side. Notice the circular arc you made with your arm. Your thumb should still be pointing forward. Do not let your arm drop.

5. Next, swing your right arm forward, so that it points straight ahead. Notice the circular arc that you made with your arm, and the new direction that your thumb is pointing. Your thumb should now be pointing left.

6. Next, swing your right arm down so that it rests at your side. Notice the circular arc you made with your arm. Your thumb will be pointing to the left. Your right arm has returned to its starting position, but your thumb is now twisted by 90 degrees. In this activity, your hand is a point moving around a sphere.

Further Research

You can find more information on the Sydney Opera House, Australia, and the world's best known structures at your local library or on the Internet.

Websites

The official website of the Sydney Opera House is www.sydneyoperahouse.com

To find out more about the city of Sydney, visit www.sydneyaustralia.com

To learn about other UNESCO World Heritage Sites, go to http://whc.unesco.org

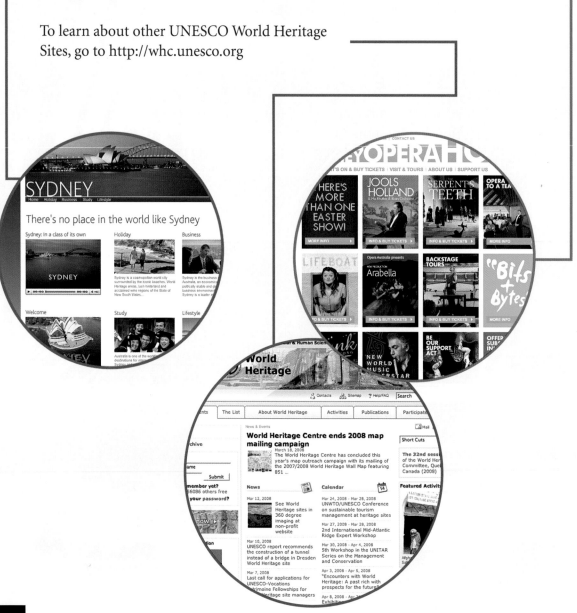

Glossary

acid rain: the result of a chemical transformation that occurs after sulfur dioxide and nitrogen oxides are emitted into the air and absorbed by water droplets in the clouds

acropolis: the fortified part of a Greek city

antiquity: of ancient times

architects: people who design buildings

cure: to make a material harden, especially concrete or cement

curvature: being curved or bent and the degree of that curve

erode: wear away

geometry: a type of mathematics that studies shapes and objects and how angles, points, lines, planes, and solids relate

icon: a symbol of great importance

innovative: featuring new and original methods and ideas

insulate: to prevent heat or sound from passing through easily

matte: a dull, lusterless finish

mausoleum: a large, detailed structure that houses a tomb

prefabricated: produced something in a standardized way, such as sections of a building, to make something before it is needed on the job site

properties: qualities or attributes

structural engineering: a profession that applies the principles of science and math to the building of structures

tiered: arranged in layers

UNESCO World Heritage Site: a site designated by the United Nations to be of great cultural worth to the world and in need of protection

vaulted: arched

weathering: the breaking down of rocks and other materials by the action of wind, rain, and other elements

Index